MW01538048

Made in the USA
Las Vegas, NV
27 March 2023

69733378R00083